PLANT BASED DIET COOKBOOK

QUICK AND EASY RECIPES

Quick, Easy and Delicious Recipes
for a lifelong Health

Amanda Grant

Copyright © 2021 by Amanda Grant

TABLE OF CONTENTS

QUICK AND EASY RECIPES

Basic Homemade Hummus

Servings: 8

Cooking Time: 10 Minutes

Ingredients:

- ➤ 1/4 cup good-quality tahini
- ➤ 2 tablespoons extra-virgin olive oil
- ➤ 1/2 teaspoon ground cumin
- ➤ 1/4 teaspoon ground bay laurel
- ➤ 1/2 teaspoon red pepper flakes
- ➤ Sea salt and ground black pepper, to taste
- ➤ 1 teaspoon dried onion powder
- ➤ 1 teaspoon parsley flakes
- ➤ 2 cloves garlic, crushed
- ➤ 2 tablespoons lemon juice
- ➤ 16 ounces chickpeas, boiled and drained

Directions:

- ➤ Blitz all the ingredients in your blender or food processor until your desired consistency is reached.
- ➤ Place in your refrigerator until ready to serve.

➢ Serve with toasted pita wedges or chips. Bon
appétit!

**Nutrition Info: Per Serving: Calories: 174; Fat:
9.1g; Carbs: 18.5g; Protein: 6.4g**

Basil Pesto Seitan Panini

Servings: 4

Cooking Time: 15 Minutes

Ingredients:

➢ For the seitan:

➢ 2/3 cup basil pesto

➢ ½ lemon, juiced

➢ 1 garlic clove, minced

➢ 1/8 tsp salt

➢ 1 cup chopped seitan

➢ For the panini:

➢ 3 tbsp basil pesto

➢ 8 thick slices whole-wheat ciabatta

➢ Olive oil for brushing

➢ 8 slices plant-based mozzarella

➢ 1 yellow bell pepper, chopped

➢ ¼ cup grated plant Parmesan cheese

Directions:

➢ In a medium bowl, mix the pesto, lemon juice, garlic, and salt. Add the seitan and coat well with the marinade. Cover with a plastic wrap and marinate in the refrigerator for 30 minutes.

➢ Preheat a large skillet over medium heat and remove the seitan from the fridge. Cook the seitan in the skillet until brown and cooked through, 3 minutes. Turn the heat off.

➢ Preheat a panini press to medium heat. In a small bowl, mix the pesto in the inner parts of two slices of bread. On the outer parts, apply some olive oil and place a slice with (the olive oil side down) in the press. Lay 2 slices of plant-based mozzarella cheese on the bread, spoon some seitan on top. Sprinkle with some bell pepper, and some plant-based Parmesan cheese. Cover with another bread slice.

➢ Close the press and grill the bread for 1 to 2 minutes. Flip the bread, and grill further for 1 minute or until the cheese melts and golden brown on both sides. Serve warm.

Nutrition Info: Per Serving: Calories: 184; Fat: 5g; Carbs: 19g; Protein: 15g

Mango & Lemon Cheesecake

Servings: 4

Cooking Time: 20 Minutes

Ingredients:

- ➤ 2/3 cup toasted rolled oats
- ➤ ¼ cup plant butter, melted
- ➤ 3 tbsp pure date sugar
- ➤ 6 oz cashew cream cheese
- ➤ ¼ cup coconut milk
- ➤ 1 lemon, zested and lemon juiced
- ➤ ¼ cup just-boiled water
- ➤ 3 tsp agar agar powder
- ➤ 1 large ripe mangoes, peeled and chopped

Directions:

- ➤ Process the oats, butter, and date sugar in a blender until smooth.
- ➤ Pour the mixture into a greased 9-inch springform pan and press the mixture onto the bottom of the pan. Refrigerate for 30 minutes until firm while you make the filling.
- ➤ In a large bowl, using an electric mixer, whisk the cashew cream cheese until smooth. Beat in the coconut milk, lemon zest, and lemon juice.

➢ Mix the boiled water and agar agar powder until dissolved and whisk this mixture into the creamy mix. Fold in the mangoes.

➢ Remove the cake pan from the fridge and pour in the mango mixture. Shake the pan to ensure a smooth layering on top. Refrigerate further for at least 3 hours.

➢ Remove the cheesecake from the fridge, release the cake pan, slice, and serve.

Nutrition Info: Per serving: Calories 337 Fats 28g Carbs 21.3g Protein 5.4g

Raspberry Protein Shake

Servings: 1

Cooking Time: 5 Minutes

Ingredients:

- ➢ ¼ avocado
- ➢ 1 c. raspberries, frozen
- ➢ 1 scoop protein powder
- ➢ ½ c. almond milk
- ➢ Ice cubes

Directions:

- ➢ In a high-speed blender add all the ingredients and blend until lumps of fruit disappear.
- ➢ Add two to four ice cubes and blend to your desired consistency.
- ➢ Serve immediately and enjoy!

Nutrition Info: Per serving: Calories: 756, Carbohydrates: 80.1 g, Proteins: 27.6 g, Fats: 40.7 g

Rice Pudding With Currants

Servings: 4

Cooking Time: 45 Minutes

Ingredients:

- ➤ 1 ½ cups water
- ➤ 1 cup white rice,2 ½ cups oat milk, divided
- ➤ 1/2 cup white sugar
- ➤ A pinch of salt, A pinch of grated nutmeg
- ➤ 1 teaspoon ground cinnamon
- ➤ 1/2 teaspoon vanilla extract
- ➤ 1/2 cup dried currants

Directions:

- ➤ In a saucepan, bring the water to a boil over medium-high heat. Immediately turn the heat to a simmer, add in the rice and let it cook for about 20 minutes. Add in the milk, sugar and spices and continue to cook for minutes more, stirring constantly to prevent the rice from sticking to the pan.
- ➤ Top with dried currants and serve at room temperature. Bon appétit!

Nutrition Info: Per Serving: Calories: 423, Fat: 5.3g, Carbs: 85g, Protein: 8.8g

Chocolate Rye Porridge

Servings: 4

Cooking Time: 10 Minutes

Ingredients:

- 2 cups rye flakes
- 2 ½ cups almond milk
- 2 ounces dried prunes, chopped
- 2 ounces dark chocolate chunks

Directions:

- Add the rye flakes and almond milk to a deep saucepan; bring to a boil over medium-high. Turn the heat to a simmer and let it cook for 5 to 6 minutes.
- Remove from the heat. Fold in the chopped prunes and chocolate chunks, gently stir to combine.
- Ladle into serving bowls and serve warm.
- Bon appétit!

Nutrition Info: Per Serving: Calories: 460, Fat: 13.1g, Carbs: 72.2g, Protein: 15g

Sweet Cornbread Muffins

Servings: 8

Cooking Time: 30 Minutes

Ingredients:

- 1 cup all-purpose flour
- 1 cup yellow cornmeal
- 1 teaspoon baking powder
- 1 teaspoon baking soda
- 1 teaspoon kosher salt
- 1/2 cup sugar
- 1/2 teaspoon ground cinnamon
- 1 1/2 cups almond milk
- 1/2 cup vegan butter, melted
- 2 tablespoons applesauce

Directions:

- Start by preheating your oven to 420 degrees F. Now, spritz a muffin tin with a nonstick cooking spray.
- In a mixing bowl, thoroughly combine the flour, cornmeal, baking soda, baking powder, salt, sugar and cinnamon.
- Gradually add in the milk, butter and applesauce, whisking constantly to avoid lumps.

➤ Scrape the batter into the prepared muffin tin. Bake your muffins for about 25 minutes or until a tester inserted in the middle comes out dry and clean.

➤ Transfer them to a wire rack to rest for minutes before unmolding and serving. Bon appétit!

Nutrition Info: Per Serving: Calories: 311, Fat: 13.7g, Carbs: 42.3g, Protein: 4.5g

Tangy Chickpea Soup With A Hint Of Lemon

Servings: 6

Cooking Time: 30 Minutes

Ingredients:

- ➢ 2 cups of freshly diced onion
- ➢ 3 freshly minced large garlic cloves
- ➢ ½ cup of freshly diced celery
- ➢ ¾ teaspoon of sea salt
- ➢ Freshly ground black pepper to taste
- ➢ 1 teaspoon of mustard seeds
- ➢ ½ teaspoon of dried oregano
- ➢ 1 teaspoon of cumin seeds
- ➢ ½ teaspoon of paprika
- ➢ 1 ½ teaspoons of dried thyme
- ➢ 3 ½ cups of cooked chickpeas
- ➢ 1 cup of dried red lentils
- ➢ 3 cups of vegetable stock
- ➢ 2 dried bay leaves
- ➢ 2 cups of freshly chopped tomatoes or zucchini
- ➢ 2 cups of water
- ➢ ¼ to 1/3 cup of fresh lemon juice

Directions:

➢ Put a large pot on the stove on medium heat.

➢ Add onion, water, salt, celery, garlic, pepper, cumin, and mustard seeds along with thyme, oregano, and paprika. Stir everything to combine well.

➢ Cover the pot and cook for about 7 minutes, stirring occasionally.

➢ Rinse the lentils.

➢ Add the lentils along with 2 ½ cups of chickpeas, zucchini/tomatoes, stock, bay leaves, and water. Stir everything to combine well.

➢ Increase the heat to bring to a boil.

➢ Once the ingredients start to boil, cover the pot, lower the heat, and simmer for 20-25 minutes.

➢ You will know that the soup is ready when the lentils are tender.

➢ After removing the bay leaves, add the lemon juice.

➢ Once the ingredients have cooled down, use a hand blender to puree the ingredients, but keep a somewhat coarse texture instead of having a smooth puree.

- ➢ Add the remaining chickpeas. Taste the soup and adjust the salt, pepper, and lemon juice to taste.
- ➢ Enjoy this amazing soup with your favorite bread.

Nutrition Info: Per Serving: Calories: 184, Fat: 7g, Carbs: 15g, Protein: 6g

Classic Pecan Pie

Servings: 4

Cooking Time: 50 Minutes

Ingredients:

- For the piecrust:
- 4 tbsp flax seed powder + 12 tbsp water
- 1/3 cup whole-wheat flour + more for dusting
- ½ tsp salt
- ¼ cup plant butter, cold and crumbled
- 3 tbsp pure malt syrup
- 1 ½ tsp vanilla extract
- For the filling:
- 3 tbsp flax seed powder + 9 tbsp water
- 2 cups toasted pecans, coarsely chopped
- 1 cup light corn syrup
- ½ cup pure date sugar
- 1 tbsp pure pomegranate molasses
- 4 tbsp plant butter, melted
- ½ tsp salt
- 2 tsp vanilla extract

Directions:

- Preheat the oven to 350 F and grease a large pie pan with cooking spray.

➢ In a medium bowl, mix the flax seed powder with water and allow thickening for 5 minutes. Do this for the filling's flax egg too in a separate bowl.

➢ In a large bowl, combine the flour and salt. Add the plant butter and using an electric hand mixer, whisk until crumbly. Pour in the crust's flax egg, maple syrup, vanilla, and mix until smooth dough forms.

➢ Flatten the dough on a flat surface, cover with plastic wrap, and refrigerate for 1 hour.

➢ After, lightly dust a working surface with flour, remove the dough onto the surface, and using a rolling pin, flatten the dough into a 1-inch diameter circle.

➢ Lay the dough on the pie pan and press to fit the shape of the pan. Use a knife to trim the edges of the pan. Lay a parchment paper on the dough, pour on some baking beans and bake in the oven until golden brown, 15 to 20 minutes. Remove the pan from the oven, pour out the baking beans, and allow cooling.

➢ In a large bowl, mix the filling's flax egg, pecans, corn syrup, date sugar, pomegranate molasses, plant butter, salt, and vanilla. Pour and spread the mixture on the piecrust. Bake further for 20 minutes or until the filling sets. Remove from the oven, decorate with more pecans, slice, and cool. Slice and serve.

Nutrition Info: Per serving: Calories 992, Fats 59.8g, Carbs 117.6 g, Protein 8g

Grilled Eggplant With Pecan Butter Sauce

Servings: 2

Cooking Time: 31 Minutes

Ingredients:

- ➤ Marinated Eggplant:
- ➤ 1 eggplant, sliced
- ➤ Salt to taste
- ➤ 4 tablespoons olive oil
- ➤ ¼ teaspoon smoked paprika
- ➤ ¼ teaspoon ground turmeric
- ➤ Black Bean and Pecan Sauce:
- ➤ ⅓ cup vegetable broth
- ➤ ⅓ cup red wine
- ➤ ⅓ cup red wine vinegar
- ➤ 1 large shallot, chopped
- ➤ 1 teaspoon ground coriander
- ➤ 2 teaspoons minced cilantro
- ➤ ½ cup pecan pieces, toasted
- ➤ 2 roasted garlic cloves
- ➤ 4 small banana peppers, seeded, and diced
- ➤ 8 tablespoons butter
- ➤ 1 tablespoon chives, chopped

> ➤ 1 (15.5 ounce) can black beans, rinsed and drained
> ➤ Salt and black pepper to taste
> ➤ 1 teaspoon fresh lime juice

Directions:

> ➤ In a saucepan, add broth, wine, vinegar, shallots, coriander, cilantro and garlic.
> ➤ Cook while stirring for minutes on a simmer.
> ➤ Meanwhile blend butter with chives, pepper, and pecans in a blender.
> ➤ Add this mixture to the broth along with salt, lime juice, black pepper, and beans.
> ➤ Mix well and cook for minutes.
> ➤ Rub the eggplant with salt and spices.
> ➤ Prepare and set up the grill over medium heat.
> ➤ Grill the eggplant slices for 6 minutes per side.
> ➤ Serve the eggplant with prepared sauce.
> ➤ Enjoy.

Nutrition Info: Per Serving: Calories: 210; Fat: 4g; Carbs: 12g; Protein: 5.2g

Cremini Mushroom Risotto

Servings: 3

Cooking Time: 20 Minutes

Ingredients:

- ➢ 3 tablespoons vegan butter
- ➢ 1 teaspoon garlic, minced
- ➢ 1 teaspoon thyme
- ➢ 1 pound Cremini mushrooms, sliced
- ➢ 1 ½ cups white rice
- ➢ 2 ½ cups vegetable broth
- ➢ 1/4 cup dry sherry wine
- ➢ Kosher salt and ground black pepper, to taste
- ➢ 3 tablespoons fresh scallions, thinly sliced

Directions:

- ➢ In a saucepan, melt the vegan butter over a moderately high flame. Cook the garlic and thyme for about minute or until aromatic.
- ➢ Add in the mushrooms and continue to sauté until they release the liquid or about 3 minutes.
- ➢ Add in the rice, vegetable broth and sherry wine. Bring to a boil; immediately turn the heat to a gentle simmer.

➢ Cook for about 15 minutes or until all the liquid has absorbed. Fluff the rice with a fork, season with salt and pepper and garnish with fresh scallions.

➢ Bon appétit!

Nutrition Info: Per Serving: Calories: 513; Fat: 12.5g; Carbs: 88g; Protein: 11.7g

Sweet Potato & Black Bean Protein Salad

Servings: 2

Cooking Time: 0 Minutes

Ingredients:

- ➤ 1 cup dry black beans
- ➤ 4 cups of spinach
- ➤ 1 medium sweet potato
- ➤ 1 cup purple onion, chopped
- ➤ 2 tbsp. olive oil
- ➤ 2 tbsp. lime juice
- ➤ 1 tbsp. minced garlic
- ➤ ½ tbsp. chili powder
- ➤ ¼ tsp. cayenne
- ➤ ¼ cup parsley
- ➤ Salt and pepper to taste

Directions:

- ➤ Prepare the black beans according to the method.
- ➤ Preheat the oven to 400°F.
- ➤ Cut the sweet potato into ¼-inch cubes and put these in a medium-sized bowl. Add the onions, 1 tablespoon of olive oil, and salt to taste.

➢ Toss the ingredients until the sweet potatoes and onions are completely coated.

➢ Transfer the ingredients to a baking sheet lined with parchment paper and spread them out in a single layer.

➢ Put the baking sheet in the oven and roast until the sweet potatoes are starting to turn brown and crispy, around 40 minutes.

➢ Meanwhile, combine the remaining olive oil, lime juice, garlic, chili powder, and cayenne thoroughly in a large bowl, until no lumps remain.

➢ Remove the sweet potatoes and onions from the oven and transfer them to the large bowl.

➢ Add the cooked black beans, parsley, and a pinch of salt.

➢ Toss everything until well combined.

➢ Then mix in the spinach, and serve in desired portions with additional salt and pepper.

➢ Store or enjoy!

Nutrition Info: Per Serving: Calories: 312; Fat: 8.1g; Carbs: 21.5g; Protein: 8.4g

Basic Homemade Tahini

Servings: 16

Cooking Time: 10 Minutes

Ingredients:

➢ 10 ounces sesame seeds, hulled

➢ 3 tablespoons canola oil

➢ 1/4 teaspoon kosher salt

Directions:

➢ Toast the sesame seeds in a nonstick skillet for about 4 minutes, stirring continuously. Cool the sesame seeds completely.

➢ Transfer the sesame seeds to the bowl of your food processor. Process for about 1 minute.

➢ Add in the oil and salt and process for a further 4 minutes, scraping down the bottom and sides of the bowl.

➢ Store your tahini in the refrigerator for up to 1 month. Bon appétit!

Nutrition Info: Per Serving: Calories: 135; Fat: 13.4g; Carbs: 2.2g; Protein: 3.6g

Pecan And Apricot Butter

Servings: 16

Cooking Time: 15 Minutes

Ingredients:

- ➢ 2 ½ cups pecans
- ➢ 1/2 cup dried apricots, chopped
- ➢ 1/2 cup sunflower oil
- ➢ 1 teaspoon bourbon vanilla
- ➢ 1/4 teaspoon ground anise
- ➢ 1/2 teaspoon cinnamon
- ➢ 1/8 teaspoon grated nutmeg
- ➢ 1/8 teaspoon salt

Directions:

- ➢ In your food processor or a high-speed blender, pulse the pecans until ground. Then, process the pecans for 5 minutes more, scraping down the sides and bottom of the bowl.
- ➢ Add in the remaining ingredients.
- ➢ Run your machine for a further 5 minutes or until the mixture is completely creamy and smooth. Enjoy!

Nutrition Info: Per Serving: Calories: 163; Fat: 17g; Carbs: 2.5g; Protein: 1.4g

Spicy Cilantro And Mint Chutney

Servings: 9

Cooking Time: 10 Minutes

Ingredients:

- ➢ 1 ½ bunches fresh cilantro
- ➢ 6 tablespoons scallions, sliced
- ➢ 3 tablespoons fresh mint leaves
- ➢ 2 jalapeno peppers, seeded
- ➢ 1/2 teaspoon kosher salt
- ➢ 2 tablespoons fresh lime juice
- ➢ 1/3 cup water

Directions:

- ➢ Place all the ingredients in the bowl of your blender or food processor.
- ➢ Then, combine the ingredients until your desired consistency has been reached.
- ➢ Bon appétit!

Nutrition Info: Per Serving: Calories: 15; Fat: 0g; Carbs: 0.9g; Protein: 0.1g

Mushroom Steak

Servings: 8

Cooking Time: 1 Hour

Ingredients:

- ➢ 1 tbsp. of the following:
- ➢ fresh lemon juice
- ➢ olive oil, extra virgin
- ➢ 2 tbsp. coconut oil
- ➢ 3 thyme sprigs
- ➢ 8 medium Portobello mushrooms
- ➢ For Sauce:
- ➢ 1 ½ t. of the following:
- ➢ minced garlic
- ➢ minced peeled fresh ginger
- ➢ 2 tbsp. of the following:
- ➢ light brown sugar
- ➢ ½ c. low-sodium soy sauce

Directions:

- ➢ For the sauce, combine all the sauce ingredients, along with ¼ cup water into a little pan and simmer to cook. Cook using a medium heat until it reduces to a glaze, approximately to 20 minutes, then remove from the heat.

➢ For the mushrooms, bring the oven to 350 heat setting.

➢ Using a skillet, melt coconut oil and olive oil, cooking the mushrooms on each side for about minutes.

➢ Next, arrange the mushrooms in a single layer on a sheet for baking and season with lemon juice, salt, and pepper.

➢ Carefully slide into the oven and roast for minutes. Let it rest for 2 minutes.

➢ Plate and drizzle the sauce over the mushrooms.

Nutrition Info: Per serving: Calories: 87, Carbohydrates: 6.2 g, Proteins: 3 g Fats: 6.2 g

Grilled Carrots With Chickpea Salad

Servings: 8

Cooking Time: 10 Minutes

Ingredients:

- ➤ 8 large carrots
- ➤ 1 tablespoon oil
- ➤ 1 ½ teaspoon salt
- ➤ 1 teaspoon dried oregano
- ➤ 1 teaspoon dried thyme
- ➤ 2 teaspoon paprika powder
- ➤ 1 ½ tablespoon soy sauce
- ➤ ½ cup of water
- ➤ Chickpea Salad
- ➤ 14 oz canned chickpeas
- ➤ 3 medium pickles
- ➤ 1 small onion
- ➤ A big handful of lettuce
- ➤ 1 teaspoon apple cider vinegar
- ➤ ½ teaspoon dried oregano
- ➤ ½ teaspoon salt
- ➤ Ground black pepper, to taste
- ➤ ½ cup vegan cream

Directions:

➤ Toss the carrots with all of its ingredients in a bowl.

➤ Thread one carrot on a stick and place it on a plate.

➤ Preheat the grill over high heat.

➤ Grill the carrots for 2 minutes per side on the grill.

➤ Toss the ingredients for the salad in a large salad bowl.

➤ Slice grilled carrots and add them on top of the salad.

➤ Serve fresh.

Nutrition Info: Per Serving: Calories: 174; Fat: 9.1g; Carbs: 18.5g; Protein: 4.4g

Parsley Pumpkin Noodles

Servings: 4

Cooking Time: 15 Minutes

Ingredients:

➢ ¼ cup plant butter

➢ ½ cup chopped onion

➢ 1 pound pumpkin, spiralized

➢ 1 bunch kale, sliced

➢ ¼ cup chopped fresh parsley

➢ Salt and black pepper to taste

Directions:

➢ Mel the butter in a skillet over medium heat. Place the onion and cook for 3 minutes. Add in pumpkin and cook for another 7-8 minutes. Stir in kale and cook for another 2 minutes, until the kale wilts. Sprinkle with parsley, salt and pepper and serve.

Nutrition Info: Per Serving: Calories: 144; Fat: 4g; Carbs: 14g; Protein: 6.4g

Sweet Potato Croutons Salad

Servings: 4

Cooking Time: 20 Minutes

Ingredients:

- ➢ 12s-ounce baked sweet potato, skin-on, cut into pieces
- ➢ 2 mandarin oranges, peeled, segmented, halved
- ➢ 1-pound mixed salad greens and vegetables
- ➢ 1 sweet apple, cored, diced, air fried
- ➢ 2 tablespoons balsamic vinegar
- ➢ 1/3 cup pomegranate seeds

Directions:

- ➢ Switch on the air fryer, insert the fryer basket, then shut it with the lid, set the frying temperature 350 degrees F, and let it preheat for 5 minutes.
- ➢ Meanwhile, prepare sweet potatoes, and for this, dice them into small pieces.
- ➢ Open the preheated fryer, place sweet potatoes in it in a single layer, spray with olive oil, close the lid and cook for 20 minutes until golden brown and cooked, shaking halfway.

➢ When done, the air fryer will beep, open the lid, and then transfer sweet potato croutons to a salad bowl.

➢ Add remaining ingredients, gently stir until combined, and then serve.

Nutrition Info: Per Serving: Calories: 280; Fat: 7.1g; Carbs: 17.5g; Protein: 8.2g

Hazelnut And Chocolate Milk

Servings: 2

Cooking Time: 0 Minute

Ingredients:

➢ 2 tablespoons cocoa powder

➢ 4 dates, pitted

➢ 1 cup hazelnuts

➢ 3 cups of water

Directions:

➢ Place all the ingredients in the order in a food processor or blender and then pulse for 2 to 3 minutes at high speed until smooth.

➢ Pour the smoothie into two glasses and then serve.

Nutrition Info: Per serving: Calories: 120 Cal, Fat: 5 g :Carbs: 19 g, Protein: 2 g, Fiber: 1 g

Mediterranean-style Zucchini Pancakes

Servings: 4

Cooking Time: 20 Minutes

Ingredients:

- ➢ 1 cup all-purpose flour
- ➢ 1/2 teaspoon baking powder
- ➢ 1/2 teaspoon dried oregano
- ➢ 1/2 teaspoon dried basil
- ➢ 1/2 teaspoon dried rosemary
- ➢ Sea salt and ground black pepper, to taste
- ➢ 1 ½ cups zucchini, grated
- ➢ 1 chia egg
- ➢ 1/2 cup rice milk
- ➢ 1 teaspoon garlic, minced
- ➢ 2 tablespoons scallions, sliced
- ➢ 4 tablespoons olive oil

Directions:

- ➢ Thoroughly combine the flour, baking powder and spices. In a separate bowl, combine the zucchini, chia egg, milk, garlic and scallions.
- ➢ Add the zucchini mixture to the dry flour mixture; stir to combine well.

➢ Then, heat the olive oil in a frying pan over a moderate flame. Cook your pancakes for 2 to minutes per side until golden brown.

➢ Bon appétit!

Nutrition Info: Per serving: Calories: 260, Fat: 14.1g, Carbs: 27.1g, Protein: 4.6g

Chocolate Mint Smoothie

Servings: 1

Cooking Time: 5 Minutes

Ingredients:

➢ 2 tbsp. sweetener of your choice

➢ 2 drops mint extract

➢ 1 tbsp. cocoa powder

➢ ½ avocado, medium

➢ ¼ c. coconut milk

➢ 1 c. almond milk, unsweetened

Directions:

➢ In a high-speed blender, add all the ingredients and blend until smooth.

➢ Add two to four ice cubes and blend.

➢ Serve immediately and enjoy!

Nutrition Info: Per serving: Calories: 401, Carbohydrates: 6.3 g, Proteins: 5 g, Fats: 40.3 g

Traditional Hanukkah Latkes

Servings: 6

Cooking Time: 30 Minutes

Ingredients:

- ➤ 1 ½ pounds potatoes, peeled, grated and drained
- ➤ 3 tablespoons green onions, sliced
- ➤ 1/3 cup all-purpose flour
- ➤ 1/2 teaspoon baking powder
- ➤ 1/2 teaspoon sea salt, preferably kala namak
- ➤ 1/4 teaspoon ground black pepper
- ➤ 1/2 olive oil,5 tablespoons applesauce
- ➤ 1 tablespoon fresh dill, roughly chopped

Directions:

- ➤ Thoroughly combine the grated potato, green onion, flour, baking powder, salt and black pepper. Preheat the olive oil in a frying pan over a moderate heat.
- ➤ Spoon 1/4 cup of potato mixture into the pan and cook your latkes until golden brown on both sides. Repeat with the remaining batter.
- ➤ Serve with applesauce and fresh dill. Bon appétit!

Nutrition Info: Per Serving: Calories: 283, Fat: 18.4g, Carbs: 27.3g, Protein: 3.2g

Fragrant Spiced Coffee

Servings: 8

Cooking Time: 3 Hours

Ingredients:

- ➢ 4 cinnamon sticks, each about 3 inches long
- ➢ 1 1/2 teaspoons of whole cloves
- ➢ 1/3 cup of honey
- ➢ 2-ounce of chocolate syrup
- ➢ 1/2 teaspoon of anise extract
- ➢ 8 cups of brewed coffee

Directions:

- ➢ Pour the coffee in a 4-quarts slow cooker and pour in the remaining ingredients except for cinnamon and stir properly.
- ➢ Wrap the whole cloves in cheesecloth and tie its corners with strings.
- ➢ Immerse this cheesecloth bag in the liquid present in the slow cooker and cover it with the lid.
- ➢ Then plug in the slow cooker and let it cook on the low heat setting for 3 hours or until heated thoroughly.

➤ When done, discard the cheesecloth bag and serve.

Nutrition Info: Calories:150 Cal, Carbohydrates:35g, Protein:3g, Fats:0g, Fiber:0g.

Ambrosia Salad With Pecans

Servings: 4

Cooking Time: 15 Minutes

Ingredients:

> ➤ 1 cup pure coconut cream, ½ tsp vanilla extract
> ➤ 2 medium bananas, peeled and cut into chunks
> ➤ 1 ½ cups unsweetened coconut flakes
> ➤ 4 tbsp toasted pecans, chopped
> ➤ 1 cup pineapple tidbits, drained
> ➤ 1 (11 oz) can mandarin oranges, drained
> ➤ ¾ cup maraschino cherries, stems removed

Directions:

> ➤ In medium bowl, mix the coconut cream and vanilla extract until well combined.
> ➤ In a larger bowl, combine the bananas, coconut flakes, pecans, pineapple, oranges, and cherries until evenly distributed.
> ➤ Pour on the coconut cream mixture and fold well into the salad.
> ➤ Chill in the refrigerator for 1 hour and serve afterwards.

Nutrition Info: Per serving: Calories 648, Fats 36g, Carbs 85.7g, Protein 6.6g

Homemade Apple Butter

Servings: 16

Cooking Time: 35 Minutes

Ingredients:

- 5 pounds apples, peeled, cored and diced
- 1 cup water
- 2/3 cup granulated brown sugar
- 1 tablespoon ground cinnamon
- 1 teaspoon ground cloves
- 1 tablespoon vanilla essence
- A pinch of freshly grated nutmeg
- A pinch of salt

Directions:

- Add the apples and water to a heavy-bottomed pot and cook for about 20 minutes.
- Then, mash the cooked apples with a potato masher; stir the sugar, cinnamon, cloves, vanilla, nutmeg and salt into the mashed apples; stir to combine well.
- Continue to simmer until the butter has thickened to your desired consistency.

Nutrition Info: Per Serving: Calories: 106, Fat: 0.3g, Carbs: 27.3g, Protein: 0.4g

White Chocolate Pudding

Servings: 4

Cooking Time: 4 Hours 20 Minutes

Ingredients:

- ➢ 3 tbsp flax seed + 9 tbsp water
- ➢ 3 tbsp cornstarch
- ➢ ¼ tbsp salt
- ➢ 1 cup cashew cream
- ➢ 2 ½ cups almond milk, ½ pure date sugar
- ➢ 1 tbsp vanilla caviar
- ➢ 6 oz unsweetened white chocolate chips
- ➢ Whipped coconut cream for topping
- ➢ Sliced bananas and raspberries for topping

Directions:

- ➢ In a small bowl, mix the flax seed powder with water and allow thickening for 5 minutes to make the flax egg.
- ➢ In a large bowl, whisk the cornstarch and salt, and then slowly mix in the in the cashew cream until smooth. Whisk in the flax egg until well combined.
- ➢ Pour the almond milk into a pot and whisk in the date sugar. Cook over medium heat while

frequently stirring until the sugar dissolves. Reduce the heat to low and simmer until steamy and bubbly around the edges.

➢ Pour half of the almond milk mixture into the flax egg mix, whisk well and pour this mixture into the remaining milk content in the pot. Whisk continuously until well combined.

➢ Bring the new mixture to a boil over medium heat while still frequently stirring and scraping all the corners of the pot, 2 minutes.

➢ Turn the heat off, stir in the vanilla caviar, then the white chocolate chips until melted. Spoon the mixture into a bowl, allow cooling for 2 minutes, cover with plastic wraps making sure to press the plastic onto the surface of the pudding, and refrigerate for 4 hours.

➢ Remove the pudding from the fridge, take off the plastic wrap and whip for about a minute.

➢ Spoon the dessert into serving cups, swirl some coconut whipping cream on top, and top with the bananas and raspberries. Enjoy immediately.

Nutrition Info: Calories 654, Fats 47.9g, Carbs 52.1g, Protein 7.3g

Oat Porridge With Almonds

Servings: 2

Cooking Time: 20 Minutes

Ingredients:

- ➤ 1 cup water
- ➤ 2 cups almond milk, divided
- ➤ 1 cup rolled oats
- ➤ 2 tablespoons coconut sugar
- ➤ 1/2 vanilla essence
- ➤ 1/4 teaspoon cardamom
- ➤ 1/2 cup almonds, chopped
- ➤ 1 banana, sliced

Directions:

- ➤ In a deep saucepan, bring the water and milk to a rapid boil. Add in the oats, cover the saucepan and turn the heat to medium.
- ➤ Add in the coconut sugar, vanilla and cardamom. Continue to cook for about 1minutes, stirring periodically.
- ➤ Spoon the mixture into serving bowls; top with almonds and banana. Bon appétit!

Nutrition Info: Per Serving: Calories: 533, Fat: 13.7g, Carbs: 85g, Protein: 21.6g

Rich Truffle Hot Chocolate

Servings: 4

Cooking Time: 2 Hours

Ingredients:

➢ 1/3 cup of cocoa powder, unsweetened

➢ 1/3 cup of coconut sugar

➢ 1/8 teaspoon of salt

➢ 1/8 teaspoon of ground cinnamon

➢ 1 teaspoon of vanilla extract, unsweetened

➢ 32 fluid ounce of coconut milk

Directions:

➢ Using a 2 quarts slow cooker, add all the ingredients and stir properly.

➢ Cover it with the lid, then plug in the slow cooker and cook it for hours on the high heat setting or until it is heated thoroughly.

➢ When done, serve right away.

Nutrition Info: Per serving: Calories:67 Cal, Carbohydrates:13g, Protein:2g, Fats:2g, Fiber:2.3g.

Apple And Cranberry Chutney

Servings: 7

Cooking Time: 1 Hour

Ingredients:

➢ 1 ½ pounds cooking apples, peeled, cored and diced 1/2 cup sweet onion, chopped

➢ 1/2 cup apple cider vinegar

➢ 1 large orange, freshly squeezed

➢ 1 cup brown sugar

➢ 1 teaspoon fennel seeds

➢ 1 tablespoon fresh ginger, peeled and grated

➢ 1 teaspoon sea salt, 1/2 cup dried cranberries

Directions:

➢ In a saucepan, place the apples, sweet onion, vinegar, orange juice, brown sugar, fennel seeds, ginger and salt. Bring the mixture to a boil.

➢ Immediately turn the heat to simmer; continue to simmer, stirring occasionally, for approximately 55 minutes, until most of the liquid has absorbed.

➢ Set aside to cool and add in the dried cranberries. Store in your refrigerator for up to 2 weeks.

Nutrition Info: Per Serving: Calories: 208, Fat: 0.3g, Carbs: 53g, Protein: 0.6g

Warm Pomegranate Punch

Servings: 10

Cooking Time: 3 Hours

Ingredients:

➤ 3 cinnamon sticks, each about 3 inches long

➤ 12 whole cloves

➤ 1/2 cup of coconut sugar

➤ 1/3 cup of lemon juice

➤ 32 fluid ounce of pomegranate juice

➤ 32 fluid ounce of apple juice, unsweetened

➤ 16 fluid ounce of brewed tea

Directions:

➤ Using a 4-quart slow cooker, pour the lemon juice, pomegranate, juice apple juice, tea, and then sugar.

➤ Wrap the whole cloves and cinnamon stick in a cheese cloth, tie its corners with a string, and immerse it in the liquid present in the slow cooker.

➤ Then cover it with the lid, plug in the slow cooker and let it cook at the low heat setting for hours or until it is heated thoroughly.

➢ When done, discard the cheesecloth bag and serve it hot or cold.

Nutrition Info: Calories:253 Cal, Carbohydrates:58g, Protein:7g, Fats:2g, Fiber:3g.

Peppery Red Lentil Spread

Servings: 9

Cooking Time: 25 Minutes

Ingredients:

- ➤ 1 ½ cups red lentils, soaked overnight and drained
- ➤ 4 ½ cups water
- ➤ 1 sprig rosemary
- ➤ 2 bay leaves
- ➤ 2 roasted peppers, seeded and diced
- ➤ 1 shallot, chopped
- ➤ 2 cloves garlic, minced
- ➤ 1/4 cup olive oil
- ➤ 2 tablespoons tahini
- ➤ Sea salt and ground black pepper, to taste

Directions:

- ➤ Add the red lentils, water, rosemary and bay leaves to a saucepan and bring to a boil over high heat. Then, turn the heat to a simmer and continue to cook for 20 minutes or until tender.
- ➤ Place the lentils in a food processor.
- ➤ Add in the remaining ingredients and process until everything is well incorporated.

➤ Bon appétit!

Nutrition Info: Per Serving: Calories: 193, Fat: 8.5g, Carbs: 22.3g, Protein: 8.5g

Nice Spiced Cherry Cider

Servings: 16

Cooking Time: 4 Hours

Ingredients:

- ➤ 2 cinnamon sticks, each about 3 inches long
- ➤ 6-ounce of cherry gelatin
- ➤ 4 quarts of apple cider

Directions:

- ➤ Using a 6-quarts slow cooker, pour the apple cider and add the cinnamon stick.
- ➤ Stir, then cover the slow cooker with its lid. Plug in the cooker and let it cook for 3 hours at the high heat setting or until it is heated thoroughly.
- ➤ Then add and stir the gelatin properly, then continue cooking for another hour.
- ➤ When done, remove the cinnamon sticks and serve the drink hot or cold.

Nutrition Info: Per serving: Calories:100 Cal, Carbohydrates:0g, Protein:0g, Fats:0g, Fiber:0g.

Cookie Dough Milkshake

Servings: 2

Cooking Time: 0 Minute

Ingredients:

- ➤ 2 tablespoons cookie dough
- ➤ 5 dates, pitted
- ➤ 2 teaspoons chocolate chips
- ➤ 1/2 teaspoon vanilla extract, unsweetened
- ➤ 1/2 cup almond milk, unsweetened
- ➤ 1 ½ cup almond milk ice cubes

Directions:

- ➤ Place all the ingredients in the order in a food processor or blender and then pulse for 2 to 3 minutes at high speed until smooth.
- ➤ Pour the milkshake into two glasses and then serve with some cookie dough balls.

Nutrition Info: Per serving: Calories: 208 Cal, Fat: 9 g, Carbs: 30 g, Protein: 2 g, Fiber: 2 g

Eggplant & Roasted Tomato Farro Salad

Servings: 3

Cooking Time: 1 Hour 30 Minutes

Ingredients:

- ➢ 4 small eggplants
- ➢ 1 ½ cups chopped cherry tomatoes
- ➢ ¾ cup uncooked faro
- ➢ 1 tablespoon olive oil
- ➢ 1 minced garlic clove
- ➢ ½ cup rinsed and drained chickpeas
- ➢ 1 tablespoon basil
- ➢ 1 tablespoon arugula
- ➢ ½ teaspoon salt and ground black pepper
- ➢ 1 tablespoon vinegar
- ➢ ½ cup toasted pine nuts

Directions:

- ➢ Preheat the oven at 300f temperature and prepare a baking sheet. Place cherry tomatoes on the baking liner and drizzle olive oil, salt, and black pepper on it and bake it for 30 to 35 minutes. Cook the faro in the salted water for 30 to 40 minutes. Slice the eggplant and salt it and leave it for 30 minutes. After that, rinse it with water and dry it kitchen towel. Now peeled and sliced the eggplants. Now place these slices on the baking liner and season it with salt, pepper and olive oil. Bake it for to 20 minutes in the preheated oven at the 450f temperature. Flip the sides of eggplant and bake it for an additional 15 to 20 minutes. Bake the pine nuts for 5 minutes and sauté the garlic. Now mix all the ingredients in a bowl and serve it.

Nutrition Info: Per serving: Carbohydrates 37g, protein 9g, fats 25g, calories 399.

Classic Onion Relish

Servings: 6

Cooking Time: 35 Minutes

Ingredients:

- ➢ 4 tablespoons vegan butter
- ➢ 1pound red onions, peeled and sliced
- ➢ 4 tablespoons granulated sugar
- ➢ 4 tablespoons white vinegar
- ➢ 1 ½ cups boiling water, 1 teaspoon sea salt
- ➢ 1 teaspoon mustard seeds 1 tps celery seeds

Directions:

- ➢ In a frying pan, melt the butter over medium-high heat. Then, sauté the onions for about 8 minutes, stirring frequently to ensure even cooking.
- ➢ Add in the sugar and continue sautéing for 5 to 6 minutes more. Add in the vinegar, boiling water, salt, mustard seeds and celery seeds.
- ➢ Turn the heat to a simmer and continue to cook, covered, for about 20 minutes.
- ➢ Remove the lid and continue to simmer until all the liquid has evaporated. Bon appétit!

Nutrition Info: Per serving: Per Serving: Calories: 118, Fat: 7.9g, Carbs: 11.3g, Protein: 0.9g

Jalapeno Rice Noodles

Servings: 4

Cooking Time: 25 Minutes

Ingredients:

- ¼ cup soy sauce
- 1 tablespoon brown sugar
- 2 teaspoons sriracha
- 3 tablespoons lime juice
- 8 oz rice noodles
- 3 teaspoons toasted sesame oil
- 1 package extra-firm tofu, pressed
- 1 onion, sliced
- 2 cups green cabbage, shredded
- 1 small jalapeno, minced
- 1 red bell pepper, sliced
- 1 yellow bell pepper, sliced
- 3 garlic cloves, minced
- 3 scallions, sliced
- 1 cup Thai basil leaves, roughly chopped
- Lime wedges for serving

Directions:

- Fill a suitably-sized pot with salted water and boil it on high heat.

➢ Add pasta to the boiling water and cook until it is al dente, then rinse under cold water.

➢ Put lime juice, soy sauce, sriracha, and brown sugar in a bowl then mix well.

➢ Place a large wok over medium heat then add 1 teaspoon sesame oil.

➢ Toss in tofu and stir for minutes until golden-brown.

➢ Transfer the golden-brown tofu to a plate and add 2 teaspoons oil to the wok.

➢ Stir in scallions, garlic, peppers, cabbage, and onion.

➢ Sauté for 2 minutes, then add cooked noodles and prepared sauce.

➢ Cook for 2 minutes, then garnish with lime wedges and basil leaves.

➢ Serve fresh.

Nutrition Info: Per serving: Per Serving:
Calories: 174, Fat: 9.1g, Carbs: 14.5g, Protein:
6.4g

Pistachio Watermelon Steak

Servings: 4

Cooking Time: 10 Minutes

Ingredients:

- ___Microgreens___
- ➢ Pistachios chopped
- ➢ Malden sea salt
- ➢ 1 tbsp. olive oil, extra virgin
- ➢ 1 watermelon
- ➢ Salt to taste

Directions:

- ➢ Begin by cutting the ends of the watermelon.
- ➢ Carefully peel the skin from the watermelon along the white outer edge.
- ➢ Slice the watermelon into 4 slices, approximately 2 inches thick.
- ➢ Trim the slices, so they are rectangular in shape approximately 2 xinches.
- ➢ Heat a skillet to medium heat add 1 tablespoon of olive oil.
- ➢ Add watermelon steaks and cook until the edges begin to caramelize.
- ➢ Plate and top with pistachios and microgreens.

➢ Sprinkle with Malden salt.

➢ Serve warm and enjoy!

Nutrition Info: Per serving: 67, Carbohydrates: 3.8 g, Proteins: 1.6 g, Fats: 5.9 g

Parsley Carrots & Parsnips

Servings: 4

Cooking Time: 25 Minutes

Ingredients:

- ➢ 2 tbsp plant butter
- ➢ ½ pound carrots, cut lengthways
- ➢ ½ pound parsnips, cut lengthways
- ➢ Salt and black pepper to taste
- ➢ ½ cup Port wine
- ➢ ¼ cup chopped fresh parsley

Directions:

- ➢ Melt the butter in a skillet over medium heat. Place in carrots and parsnips and cook for 5 minutes, stirring occasionally. Sprinkle with salt and pepper. Pour in Port wine and ¼ cup water. Lower the heat and simmer for minutes. Uncover and increase the heat. Cook until forms a syrupy sauce. Remove to a bowl and serve garnished with parsley.

Nutrition Info: Per Serving: Calories: 94, Fat: 1.1g, Carbs: 6g, Protein: 3g

Cashew Cream Cheese

Servings: 6

Cooking Time: 10 Minutes

Ingredients:

➢ 1 ½ cups cashews, soaked overnight and drained

➢ 1/3 cup water

➢ 1/4 teaspoon coarse sea salt

➢ 1/4 teaspoon dried dill weed

➢ 1/4 teaspoon garlic powder

➢ 2 tablespoons nutritional yeast

➢ 2 probiotic capsules

Directions:

➢ Process the cashews and water in your blender until creamy and uniform.

➢ Add in the salt, dill, garlic powder and nutritional yeast; continue to blend until everything is well incorporated.

➢ Spoon the mixture into a sterilized glass jar. Add in the probiotic powder and combine with a wooden spoon (not metal!

➢ Cover the jar with a clean kitchen towel and let it stand on the kitchen counter to ferment for 248 hours.

➢ Keep in your refrigerator for up to a week. Bon appétit!

Nutrition Info: Per Serving: Calories: 197, Fat: 14.4g, Carbs: 11.4g, Protein: 7.4g

Avocado And Roasted Beet Salad

Servings: 2

Cooking Time: 40 Minutes

Ingredients:

- ➤ 2 beets, thinly sliced and peeled
- ➤ 1 teaspoon of olive oil
- ➤ A pinch of sea salt
- ➤ 1 avocado
- ➤ 2 cups of mixed greens
- ➤ 4 tablespoons of creamy Balsamic Dressing
- ➤ 2 tablespoons of chopped almonds

Directions:

- ➤ Prepare the oven by preheating it to 450 degrees F.
- ➤ In a large bowl, combine the oil, beets and salt, massage with your hands.
- ➤ Arrange the beets in a single layer on a baking dish and bake them for minutes.
- ➤ Slice the avocado in half and remove the seed.
- ➤ Scoop out the avocado flesh in one piece and slice it into crescents.
- ➤ Once the beets are cooked, remove them from the oven and arrange the slices onto plates.

➢ Top the beets with a slice of avocado, a handful of salad and drizzle the dressing over the top, coat with some chopped almonds and serve.

Nutrition Info: Per Serving: Calories: 190, Fat: 9.1g, Carbs: 18.5g, Protein: 6.4g

Vegan Bake Pasta With Bolognese Sauce And Cashew Cream

Servings: 8

Cooking Time: 20 Minutes

Ingredients:

- ➢ For the Pasta:
- ➢ 1 packet penne pasta
- ➢ For the Bolognese Sauce:
- ➢ 1 tablespoon soy sauce
- ➢ 1 small can lentils
- ➢ 1 tablespoon brown sugar
- ➢ ½ cup tomato paste
- ➢ 1 teaspoon garlic, crushed
- ➢ 1 tablespoon olive oil
- ➢ 2 tomatoes, chopped
- ➢ 1 onion, chopped
- ➢ 2 cups mushrooms, sliced
- ➢ Salt, to taste
- ➢ Pepper, to taste
- ➢ For the Cashew Cream:
- ➢ 1 cup raw cashews
- ➢ ½ lemon, squeezed
- ➢ ½ teaspoon salt

- ½ cup water
- For the White Sauce:
- 1 teaspoon black pepper
- 1 teaspoon Dijon mustard
- ¼ cup nutritional yeast
- Sea salt, as required
- 2 cups coconut milk
- 3 tablespoons vegan butter
- 2 tablespoons all-purpose flour
- 1/3 cup vegetable broth

Directions:

- Take a pot and boil water, add pasta to it, boil for 3 minutes and set aside.
- Fry onion and garlic, mushroom in olive oil and add soy sauce to it.
- Add in sugar tomato paste, lentils, and canned tomato to it and let it simmer, Bolognese sauce is prepared.
- Season it with salt and black pepper.
- Add the lemon juice, cashews, water and salt to the blender, blend for 2 minutes.
- Add this to the sauce you have prepared and stir pasta in it.

- ➢ Melt the vegan butter in a saucepan, add in the flour and stir.
- ➢ Add vegetable stock and coconut milk to it and whisk well.
- ➢ Stir continuously and let it boil for about 5 minutes, then remove from heat.
- ➢ Add Dijon mustard, nutritional yeast, black pepper, and sea salt.
- ➢ Preheat the oven to 430 degrees F.
- ➢ Prepare rectangular oven-safe dish by placing pasta and Bolognese sauce to it.
- ➢ Pour the white sauce on it and bake for a time period of 20-25 minutes.

Nutrition Info: Per Serving: Calories: 214, Fat: 6.1g, Carbs: 17.5g, Protein: 6.4g

Zesty Rice Bowls With Tempeh

Servings: 4

Cooking Time: 50 Minutes

Ingredients:

- ➢ 2 tbsp olive oil
- ➢ 1 ½ cups crumbled tempeh
- ➢ 1 tsp Creole seasoning
- ➢ 2 red bell peppers, sliced
- ➢ 1 cup brown rice
- ➢ 2 cups vegetable broth
- ➢ Salt to taste
- ➢ 1 lemon, zested and juiced
- ➢ 1 (8 oz) can black beans, drained
- ➢ 2 chives, chopped
- ➢ 2 tbsp freshly chopped parsley

Directions:

- ➢ Heat the olive oil in a medium pot and cook in the tempeh until golden brown, 5 minutes. Season with the Creole seasoning and stir in the bell peppers. Cook until the peppers slightly soften, 3 minutes. Stir in the brown rice, vegetable broth, salt, and lemon zest. Cover and cook until the rice is tender and all the liquid is absorbed, to 25 minutes. Mix in the lemon juice, beans, and chives. Allow warming for 3 to 5 minutes and dish the food. Garnish with the parsley and serve warm.

Nutrition Info: Per Serving: Calories: 224, Fat: 6.1g, Carbs: 14.5g, Protein: 11g

Butternut Squash Steak

Servings: 4

Cooking Time: 50 Minutes

Ingredients:

- 2 tbsp. coconut yogurt
- ½ t. sweet paprika
- 1 ¼ c. low-sodium vegetable broth
- 1 sprig thyme
- 1 finely chopped garlic clove
- 1 big thinly sliced shallot
- 1 tbsp. margarine
- 2 tbsp. olive oil, extra virgin
- Salt and pepper to liking

Directions:

- Bring the oven to 375 heat setting.
- Cut the squash, lengthwise, into 4 steaks.
- Carefully core one side of each squash with a paring knife in a crosshatch pattern.
- Using a brush, coat with olive oil each side of the steak then season generously with salt and pepper.
- In an oven-safe, non-stick skillet, bring 2 tablespoons of olive oil to a warm temperature.

➢ Place the steaks on the skillet with the cored side down and cook at medium temperature until browned, approximately 5 minutes.

➢ Flip and repeat on the other side for about 3 minutes.

➢ Place the skillet into the oven to roast the squash for 7 minutes.

➢ Take out from the oven, placing on a plate and covering with aluminum foil to keep warm.

➢ Using the previously used skillet, add thyme, garlic, and shallot, cooking at medium heat. Stir frequently for about 2 minutes.

➢ Add brandy and cook for an additional minute.

➢ Next, add paprika and whisk the mixture together for 3 minutes.

➢ Add in the yogurt seasoning with salt and pepper.

➢ Plate the steaks and spoon the sauce over the top.

➢ Garnish with parsley and enjoy!

Nutrition Info: Calories: 300, Carbohydrates: 46 g, Proteins: 5.3 g, Fats: 10.6g

Harissa Bulgur Bowl

Servings: 4

Cooking Time: 25 Minutes

Ingredients:

- ➤ 1 cup bulgur wheat
- ➤ 1 ½ cups vegetable broth
- ➤ 2 cups sweet corn kernels, thawed
- ➤ 1 cup canned kidney beans, drained
- ➤ 1 red onion, thinly sliced
- ➤ 1 garlic clove, minced
- ➤ Sea salt and ground black pepper, to taste
- ➤ 1/4 cup harissa paste
- ➤ 1 tablespoon lemon juice
- ➤ 1 tablespoon white vinegar
- ➤ 1/4 cup extra-virgin olive oil
- ➤ 1/4 cup fresh parsley leaves, roughly chopped

Directions:

- ➤ In a deep saucepan, bring the bulgur wheat and vegetable broth to a simmer; let it cook, covered, for to 13 minutes.
- ➤ Let it stand for 5 to 10 minutes and fluff your bulgur with a fork.

> ➤ Add the remaining ingredients to the cooked bulgur wheat; serve warm or at room temperature. Bon appétit!

Nutrition Info: Per Serving: Calories: 353, Fat: 15.5g, Carbs: 48.5g, Protein: 8.4g

Pungent Mushroom Barley Risotto

Servings: 4

Cooking Time: 3 Hours And 9 Minutes

Ingredients:

- ➢ 1 1/2 cups of hulled barley, rinsed and soaked overnight
- ➢ 8 ounces of carrots, peeled and chopped
- ➢ 1 pound of mushrooms, sliced
- ➢ 1 large white onion, peeled and chopped
- ➢ 3/4 teaspoon of salt
- ➢ 1/2 teaspoon of ground black pepper
- ➢ 4 sprigs thyme
- ➢ 1/4 cup of chopped parsley
- ➢ 2/3 cup of grated vegan Parmesan cheese
- ➢ 1 tablespoon of apple cider vinegar
- ➢ 2 tablespoons of olive oil
- ➢ 1 1/2 cups of vegetable broth

Directions:

- ➢ Place a large non-stick skillet pan over a medium-high heat, add the oil and let it heat until it gets hot.
- ➢ Add the onion along with 1/4 teaspoon of each the salt and black pepper.

➢ Cook it for 5 minutes or until it turns golden brown.

➢ Then add the mushrooms and continue cooking for 2 minutes.

➢ Add the barley, thyme and cook for another 2 minutes.

➢ Transfer this mixture to a quarts slow cooker and add the carrots, 1/4 teaspoon of salt, and the vegetable broth.

➢ Stir properly and cover it with the lid.

➢ Plug in the slow cooker, let it cook for 3 hours at the high heat setting or until the grains absorb all the cooking liquid and the vegetables get soft.

➢ Remove the thyme sprigs, pour in the remaining ingredients except for parsley and stir properly.

➢ Pour in the warm water and stir properly until the risotto reaches your desired state.

➢ Add the seasoning, then garnish it with parsley and serve.

Nutrition Info: Per serving: Calories:321 Cal, Carbohydrates:48g, Protein:12g, Fats:10g, Fiber:11g.

Breaded Tofu Steaks

Servings: 4

Cooking Time: 12 Minutes

Ingredients:

- 3 cups (750 grams) tofu, extra-firm, pressed
- 4 tablespoons tomato paste
- 2 ½ tablespoons minced garlic
- 1 cup (236 grams) panko breadcrumbs and more as needed
- ½ teaspoon ground black pepper
- 2 tablespoon maple syrup
- 2 tablespoon Dijon mustard
- 2 tablespoon soy sauce
- 4 tablespoons olive oil
- 2 tablespoon water
- BBQ sauce for serving

Directions:

- Prepare the tofu steaks: pat dry tofu and then cut them into four slices.
- Prepare the sauce: take a medium bowl, add garlic, black pepper, maple syrup, mustard, tomato paste, soy sauce, and water; stir until combined.

➢ Take a shallow dish and place bread crumbs on it.

➢ Working on one tofu steak at a time, first coat it with prepared sauce, then dredge it with bread crumbs until evenly coated and place it on a plate.

➢ Repeat with the remaining tofu slices.

➢ Take a frying pan, place it over medium heat, pour oil in it and when hot, place a tofu steak inside and cook for 4 to minutes per side until golden brown and cooked.

➢ Transfer tofu steak to a plate and repeat with the remaining tofu steaks.

➢ Serve tofu steaks with the BBQ sauce.

Nutrition Info: Per serving: 419.4 Cal; 23.9 g Fat; 3.9 g Saturated Fat; 33.3 g Carbs; 4.3 g Fiber; 22.8 g Protein; 3 g Sugar;

Aromatic Rice Pudding With Dried Figs

Servings: 4

Cooking Time: 45 Minutes

Ingredients:

- ➤ 2 cups water,1 cup medium-grain white rice
- ➤ 3 ½ cups coconut milk, 1/2 cup coconut sugar
- ➤ 1 cinnamon stick, 1 vanilla bean
- ➤ 1/2 cup dried figs, chopped
- ➤ 4 tablespoons coconut, shredded

Directions:

- ➤ In a saucepan, bring the water to a boil over medium-high heat. Immediately turn the heat to a simmer, add in the rice and let it cook for about 20 minutes.
- ➤ Add in the milk, sugar and spices and continue to cook for minutes more, stirring constantly to prevent the rice from sticking to the pan.
- ➤ Top with dried figs and coconut; serve your pudding warm or at room temperature. Bon appétit!

Nutrition Info: Per serving: Per Serving: Calories: 407, Fat: 7.5g, Carbs: 74.3g, Protein: 10.7g

Overnight Oatmeal With Prunes

Servings: 2

Cooking Time: 5 Minutes

Ingredients:

➢ 1 cup hemp milk

➢ 1 tablespoon flax seed, ground

➢ 2/3 cup rolled oats

➢ 2 ounces prunes, sliced

➢ 2 tablespoons agave syrup

➢ A pinch of salt

➢ 1/2 teaspoon ground cinnamon

Directions:

➢ Divide the ingredients, except for the prunes, between two mason jars.

➢ Cover and shake to combine well. Let them sit overnight in your refrigerator.

➢ Garnish with sliced prunes just before serving. Enjoy!

Nutrition Info: Per Serving: Calories: 398, Fat: 9.9g, Carbs: 66.2g, Protein: 13.7g

Chickpea Garden Vegetable Medley

Servings: 4

Cooking Time: 30 Minutes

Ingredients:

- 2 tablespoons olive oil
- 1 onion, finely chopped
- 1 bell pepper, chopped
- 1 fennel bulb, chopped
- 3 cloves garlic, minced
- 2 ripe tomatoes, pureed
- 2 tablespoons fresh parsley, roughly chopped
- 2 tablespoons fresh basil, roughly chopped
- 2 tablespoons fresh coriander, roughly chopped
- 2 cups vegetable broth
- 14 ounces canned chickpeas, drained
- Kosher salt and ground black pepper, to taste
- 1/2 teaspoon cayenne pepper
- 1 teaspoon paprika
- 1 avocado, peeled and sliced

Directions:

- In a heavy-bottomed pot, heat the olive oil over medium heat. Once hot, sauté the onion, bell pepper and fennel bulb for about 4 minutes.

➢ Sauté the garlic for about 1 minute or until aromatic.

➢ Add in the tomatoes, fresh herbs, broth, chickpeas, salt, black pepper, cayenne pepper and paprika. Let it simmer, stirring occasionally, for about 20 minutes or until cooked through.

➢ Taste and adjust the seasonings. Serve garnished with the slices of the fresh avocado. Bon appétit!

Nutrition Info: Per Serving: Calories: 369, Fat: 18.1g, Carbs: 43.5g, Protein: 13.2g

Mediterranean Tomato Gravy

Servings: 6

Cooking Time: 20 Minutes

Ingredients:

- ➤ 3 tablespoons olive oil
- ➤ 1 red onion, chopped
- ➤ 3 cloves garlic, crushed
- ➤ 4 tablespoons cornstarch
- ➤ 1 can (14 ½-ounce tomatoes, crushed
- ➤ 1/2 teaspoon dried basil
- ➤ 1/2 teaspoon dried oregano
- ➤ 1/2 teaspoon dried thyme
- ➤ 1 teaspoon dried parsley flakes
- ➤ Sea salt and black pepper, to taste

Directions:

- ➤ Heat the olive oil in a large saucepan over medium-high heat. Once hot, sauté the onion and garlic until tender and fragrant.
- ➤ Add in the cornstarch and continue to cook for 1 minute more.
- ➤ Add in the canned tomatoes and bring to a boil over medium-high heat; stir in the spices and turn the heat to a simmer.

➢ Let it simmer for about 10 minutes until everything is cooked through.

➢ Serve with vegetables of choice. Bon appétit!

Nutrition Info: Per Serving: Calories: 106, Fat: 6.6g, Carbs: 9.6g, Protein: 0.8g

Mediterranean-style Rice

Servings: 4

Cooking Time: 20 Minutes

Ingredients:

- ➤ 3 tablespoons vegan butter, at room temperature
- ➤ 4 tablespoons scallions, chopped
- ➤ 2 cloves garlic, minced
- ➤ 1 bay leaf
- ➤ 1 thyme sprig, chopped
- ➤ 1 rosemary sprig, chopped
- ➤ 1 ½ cups white rice
- ➤ 2 cups vegetable broth
- ➤ 1 large tomato, pureed
- ➤ Sea salt and ground black pepper, to taste
- ➤ 2 ounces Kalamata olives, pitted and sliced

Directions:

- ➤ In a saucepan, melt the vegan butter over a moderately high flame. Cook the scallions for about 2 minutes or until tender.
- ➤ Add in the garlic, bay leaf, thyme and rosemary and continue to sauté for about 1 minute or until aromatic.

➢ Add in the rice, broth and pureed tomato. Bring to a boil; immediately turn the heat to a gentle simmer.

➢ Cook for about 15 minutes or until all the liquid has absorbed. Fluff the rice with a fork, season with salt and pepper and garnish with olives; serve immediately.

➢ Bon appétit!

Nutrition Info: Per Serving: Calories: 403, Fat: 12g, Carbs: 64.1g, Protein: 8.3g

Teff Salad With Avocado And Beans

Servings: 2

Cooking Time: 20 Minutes

Ingredients:

- ➤ 2 cups water, 1/2 cup teff grain
- ➤ 1 teaspoon fresh lemon juice
- ➤ 3 tablespoons vegan mayonnaise
- ➤ 1 teaspoon deli mustard
- ➤ 1 small avocado, pitted, peeled and sliced
- ➤ 1 small red onion, thinly sliced
- ➤ 1 small Persian cucumber, sliced
- ➤ 1/2 cup canned kidney beans, drained
- ➤ 2 cups baby spinach

Directions:

- ➤ In a deep saucepan, bring the water to a boil over high heat. Add in the teff grain and turn the heat to a simmer.
- ➤ Continue to cook, covered, for about minutes or until tender. Let it cool completely.
- ➤ Add in the remaining ingredients and toss to combine. Serve at room temperature.

Nutrition Info: Per Serving: Calories: 463, Fat: 21.2g, Carbs: 58.9g, Protein: 13.1g

Chocolate And Cherry Smoothie

Servings: 2

Cooking Time: 0 Minute

Ingredients:

- ➢ 4 cups frozen cherries
- ➢ 2 tablespoons cocoa powder
- ➢ 1 scoop of protein powder
- ➢ 1 teaspoon maple syrup
- ➢ 2 cups almond milk, unsweetened

Directions:

- ➢ Place all the ingredients in the order in a food processor or blender and then pulse for 2 to 3 minutes at high speed until smooth.
- ➢ Pour the smoothie into two glasses and then serve.

Nutrition Info: Calories: 324 Cal, Fat: 5 g :Carbs: 75.1 g, Protein: 7.2 g, Fiber: 11.3 g

Overnight Oatmeal With Walnuts

Servings: 3

Cooking Time: 5 Minutes

Ingredients:

➤ 1 cup old-fashioned oats

➤ 3 tablespoons chia seeds

➤ 1 ½ cups coconut milk

➤ 3 teaspoons agave syrup

➤ 1 teaspoon vanilla extract

➤ 1/2 teaspoon ground cinnamon

➤ 3 tablespoons walnuts, chopped

➤ A pinch of salt

➤ A pinch of grated nutmeg

Directions:

➤ Divide the ingredients between three mason jars.

➤ Cover and shake to combine well. Let them sit overnight in your refrigerator.

➤ You can add some extra milk before serving. Enjoy!

Nutrition Info: Per Serving: Calories: 423, Fat: 16.8g, Carbs: 53.1g,Protein: 17.3g

Anasazi Bean And Vegetable Stew

Servings: 3

Cooking Time: 1 Hour

Ingredients:

> 1 cup Anasazi beans, soaked overnight and drained
> 3 cups roasted vegetable broth
> 1 bay laurel
> 1 thyme sprig, chopped
> 1 rosemary sprig, chopped
> 3 tablespoons olive oil
> 1 large onion, chopped
> 2 celery stalks, chopped
> 2 carrots, chopped
> 2 bell peppers, seeded and chopped
> 1 green chili pepper, seeded and chopped
> 2 garlic cloves, minced
> Sea salt and ground black pepper, to taste
> 1 teaspoon cayenne pepper
> 1 teaspoon paprika

Directions:

> In a saucepan, bring the Anasazi beans and broth to a boil. Once boiling, turn the heat to a simmer.

Add in the bay laurel, thyme and rosemary; let it cook for about 50 minutes or until tender.

➢ Meanwhile, in a heavy-bottomed pot, heat the olive oil over medium-high heat. Now, sauté the onion, celery, carrots and peppers for about 4 minutes until tender.

➢ Add in the garlic and continue to sauté for seconds more or until aromatic.

➢ Add the sautéed mixture to the cooked beans. Season with salt, black pepper, cayenne pepper and paprika.

➢ Continue to simmer, stirring periodically, for 10 minutes more or until everything is cooked through. Bon appétit!

Nutrition Info: Per Serving: Calories: 444, Fat: 15.8g, Carbs: 58.2g, Protein: 20.2g

Mexican-style Bean Bowl

Servings: 6

Cooking Time: 1 Hour

Ingredients:

➤ 1 pound red beans, soaked overnight and drained

➤ 1 cup canned corn kernels, drained

➤ 2 roasted bell peppers, sliced

➤ 1 chili pepper, finely chopped

➤ 1 cup cherry tomatoes, halved

➤ 1 red onion, chopped

➤ 1/4 cup fresh cilantro, chopped

➤ 1/4 cup fresh parsley, chopped

➤ 1 teaspoon Mexican oregano

➤ 1/4 cup red wine vinegar

➤ 2 tablespoons fresh lemon juice

➤ 1/3 cup extra-virgin olive oil

➤ Sea salt and ground black, to taste

➤ 1 avocado, peeled, pitted and sliced

Directions:

➤ Cover the soaked beans with a fresh change of cold water and bring to a boil. Let it boil for about minutes. Turn the heat to a simmer and continue to cook for 50 to 55 minutes or until tender.

➢ Allow your beans to cool completely, then, transfer them to a salad bowl.

➢ Add in the remaining ingredients and toss to combine well. Serve at room temperature.

➢ Bon appétit!

Nutrition Info: Per Serving: Calories: 465, Fat: 17.9g, Carbs: 60.4g, Protein: 20.2g

Chocolate Smoothie

Servings: 2

Cooking Time: 5 Minutes

Ingredients:

- ¼ c. almond butter
- ¼ c. cocoa powder, unsweetened
- ½ c. coconut milk, canned
- 1 c. almond milk, unsweetened

Directions:

- Before making the smoothie, freeze the almond milk into cubes using an ice cube tray. This would take a few hours, so prepare it ahead.
- Blend everything using your preferred machine until it reaches your desired thickness.
- Serve immediately and enjoy!

Nutrition Info: Calories: 147, Carbohydrates: 8.2 g, Proteins: 4 g, Fats: 13.4 g

Easy Barley Risotto

Servings: 4

Cooking Time: 35 Minutes

Ingredients:

- ➢ 2 tablespoons vegan butter
- ➢ 1 medium onion, chopped
- ➢ 1 bell pepper, seeded and chopped
- ➢ 2 garlic cloves, minced
- ➢ 1 teaspoon ginger, minced
- ➢ 2 cups vegetable broth
- ➢ 2 cups water
- ➢ 1 cup medium pearl barley
- ➢ 1/2 cup white wine
- ➢ 2 tablespoons fresh chives, chopped

Directions:

- ➢ Melt the vegan butter in a saucepan over medium-high heat.
- ➢ Once hot, cook the onion and pepper for about 3 minutes until just tender.
- ➢ Add in the garlic and ginger and continue to sauté for 2 minutes or until aromatic.
- ➢ Add in the vegetable broth, water, barley and wine; cover and continue to simmer for about 30

minutes. Once all the liquid has been absorbed; fluff the barley with a fork.

➢ Garnish with fresh chives and serve warm. Bon appétit!

Nutrition Info: Per Serving: Calories: 269, Fat: 7.1g, Carbs: 43.9g, Protein: 8g

Vegan Ricotta Cheese

Servings: 12

Cooking Time: 10 Minutes

Ingredients:

- ➤ 1/2 cup raw cashew nuts, soaked overnight and drained
- ➤ 1/2 cup raw sunflower seeds, soaked overnight and drained
- ➤ 1/4 cup water
- ➤ 1 heaping tablespoon coconut oil, melted
- ➤ 1 tablespoon lime juice, freshly squeezed
- ➤ 1 tablespoon white vinegar
- ➤ 1/4 teaspoon Dijon mustard
- ➤ 2 tablespoons nutritional yeast
- ➤ 1/2 teaspoon garlic powder
- ➤ 1/2 teaspoon turmeric powder
- ➤ 1/2 teaspoon salt

Directions:

- ➤ Process the cashews, sunflower seeds and water in your blender until creamy and uniform.
- ➤ Add in the remaining ingredients; continue to blend until everything is well incorporated.

➢ Keep in your refrigerator for up to a week. Bon appétit!

Nutrition Info: Per Serving: Calories: 74, Fat: 6.3g, Carbs: 3.3g, Protein: 2.7g